HOW TO TIDY YOUR MIND

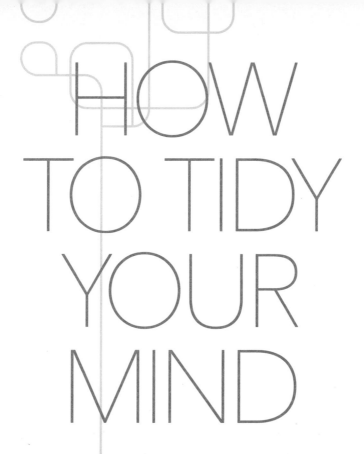

HOW TO TIDY YOUR MIND

Tips and Techniques to Help You Reduce Mental Clutter

ANNA BARNES

Andrews McMeel
PUBLISHING®

Andrews McMeel Publishing
a division of Andrews McMeel Universal
1130 Walnut Street
Kansas City, Missouri 64106

www.andrewsmcmeel.com

23 24 25 26 27 CHJ 10 9 8 7 6 5 4 3 2 1

ISBN: 978-1-5248-8359-1

Library of Congress Control Number:
2022947233

Editor: Marya Pasciuto
Art Director/Designer: Diane Marsh
Production Editor: Meg Utz
Production Manager: Chadd Keim

CONTENTS

INTRODUCTION

If your mind feels like a cluttered mess, you're not alone. This busy, modern world is full of things requiring our attention, and inevitably some of these find their way into our consciousness and set up camp, whether we have invited them or not. They then accumulate and clog up our minds, making it difficult to make decisions and deal with daily tasks. However, it's your mind and you're the boss! Learning how to declutter it will not only give you the space to think more clearly but will also help you to feel more positive and joyful and be better able to handle day-to-day life. It's time to embark on your journey from mental clutter to mental clarity.

Simplicity
boils down
to two things:
identify the
essential &
eliminate
the rest.

LEO BABAUTA

CHAPTER ONE

WHAT IS MENTAL CLUTTER?

Mental clutter is a term used to describe unhelpful thoughts and feelings that can take up space in your mind, making you feel tired and foggy. It can affect your mood and performance and can hinder your daily life, draining your energy and making you feel fed up and frazzled. It refers to all those unresolved thoughts and tasks that might seem small on their own, but that can build up to create a feeling of not being in control of your life. So, what better time to begin clearing that mental clutter than right now?

INFO
OVERLOAD

The term "information overload" refers to those times when your mind is swamped with stimuli competing for your attention. Your phone buzzes with notifications, messages arrive in your inbox, multiple tabs are open in your browser, a pile of mail awaits, you have a phone call to make, you remember it's a friend's birthday, there's nothing in the fridge for dinner, and you notice the time and have to rush out to an appointment.

This modern world is busy, so it's no wonder many of us end up feeling worn out with all these demands on our time and attention. Excessive stimulation can increase our brain's production of the stress hormone cortisol, as well as adrenaline, which causes the fight, flight, or freeze response—your body's automatic reaction to fear. Information overload can also lead to a fatigued thinking state, where the sheer number of thoughts you have impairs your overall decisiveness and decision-making. It's like a pile-up of unimportant decisions that distract you from the giant semi truck—the important decision—that really does require your attention.

PROLONGED STRESS

Humans are primed to deal with stress—up to a certain point. A little stress—or mental arousal—stimulates us to go out, find food and shelter, take measured risks to ensure our survival, and connect with others. However, when the stress doesn't abate and your brain is still pumping out fight-or-flight hormones when there's no danger, you can become overstimulated and exhausted. Chronic stress can lead to anxiety, fatigue, irritability, digestive issues, and trouble sleeping. Decluttering your mind can help to eliminate the unnecessary stress in your life, helping you feel calmer and more clear-headed.

Turn your wounds into wisdom.

OPRAH WINFREY

BRAIN
FOG

A pile-up of small stimuli overloading our minds can lead to us neglecting the bigger issues that really matter. If this imbalance isn't managed, it can escalate and lead to anxiety, exhaustion, low energy, forgetfulness, and fuzzy thinking and in turn can result in rushed decisions. This inability to focus or think straight is sometimes referred to as "brain fog," and it's a metaphorical red flag, alerting us to the need to address our mental clutter and work out what's causing it, so we can take steps to alleviate it.

Start where you are.
Use what you have.
Do what you can.

ARTHUR ASHE

Clutter is
postponed
decisions.

BARBARA HEMPHILL

THE
TROUBLE
WITH
MULTITASKING

Multitasking means tackling multiple tasks at the same time. However, research suggests it is more effective to approach one thing at a time. Rapidly switching between several tasks uses up more mental energy and can make multitaskers feel distracted and unable to focus. Rather than making us more productive, attempting to juggle too many jobs at once actually means each task takes longer and can leave us feeling stressed and overwhelmed.

ZEIGARNIK EFFECT

Russian psychologist Bluma Zeigarnik observed that waiters recalled orders they had yet to fulfill better than those they'd already served. This led to the theory of the Zeigarnik effect, where people spend more mental energy focusing on unfinished or interrupted tasks than they do on completed ones. Uncompleted tasks create cognitive demand, requiring mental effort to keep them at the front of our minds. Once fulfilled, we can tick off these items and mentally relax. This phenomenon explains why it's so stressful to keep a mental to-do list cluttering up your mind. The lesson? Avoid procrastinating and work through that to-do list.

"LITTLE AND OFTEN" IS THE MOST EFFECTIVE APPROACH FOR A HAPPY MIND

JUST
DO IT!

Procrastination is a common cause of mental clutter. Continually putting off decisions and tasks instead of tackling them—especially if it involves something challenging, or something that you feel is stressful—not only lengthens the to-do list floating around your head but can also leave you feeling anxious. After all, now you have not only the task itself in your mind but also the stress of thinking about it and remembering to do it. Procrastination is often avoidance. Sometimes, the best approach is simply to tackle that task.

The secret of
getting ahead
is getting
started.

MARK TWAIN

RECOGNIZING THE SIGNS

You've heard of burnout or nervous breakdowns, when people—often extremely capable people who appear to effortlessly juggle multiple demands—suddenly hit a proverbial wall. This is the extreme of what can happen when we ignore our mental clutter and don't listen to our stress signals. Signs that you are approaching burnout include trouble sleeping, difficulty concentrating, and taking longer than usual to complete tasks, as well as feeling drained, overloaded, irritable, or withdrawn.

Learning to recognize the signs that your mind is becoming a congested place is a vital step toward acknowledging—and then tackling—that clutter. Be alert to the times when you're feeling slow, tired, or heavy, or periods when the days seem to be piling up with a never-ending list of things to do. When this happens, pause, prioritize your self-care, and ask friends and family for support in sharing out tasks. Delegating small jobs to others and cutting back non-essential commitments will give you the space and energy to rebuild your reserves.

Keep your
eyes on the
finish line
and not on
the turmoil
around you.

RIHANNA

TOO MUCH NOISE

When your mind is brimful of clutter or "noise," it can be difficult to remain focused on a particular task for any length of time. This can become incredibly frustrating. It makes perfect sense, though. Imagine you have been asked to babysit a child—but when you arrive, there are fifty children needing your care and attention! Help! Keeping your mind tidy and clutter-free can focus your attention and help you stay productive.

Clutter isn't just the stuff on the floor. It's anything that gets between you and the life you want to be living.

PETER WALSH

BE KIND
TO YOUR
MIND

Humans have evolved over millions of years to become excellent at hunting, foraging, and surviving. We are also skilled at adapting, but many of the stimuli present in our modern lives are so recent—the blink of an eye in evolutionary terms—that it's not surprising our brains are struggling to catch up with and assimilate all this busyness. So, be kind to your mind and give it a rest from all the excess stimulation by learning to slow down and declutter your thoughts.

EVERYTHING
CAN BE DONE
ONE STEP
AT A TIME

MAKE A
VOW TO
YOURSELF

Think of the people in your life and all the ways in which you demonstrate your commitment to them—listening to them, taking them places, cooking for them, doing things to support them, and showing you care.

Now shine the spotlight on yourself. Do you show yourself the same level of commitment?

If the answer is no, ask yourself why this might be. Don't you deserve the same respect and care that you give to others?

Consciously choosing to commit to yourself is a powerful way to take responsibility and show compassion to yourself, and to get your life in order. Making this pledge is hugely empowering and astonishingly effective—a psychological first step in taking better care of yourself. You could sign up for a class that you'd really enjoy, or block off an hour to yourself when your family's not allowed to interrupt you.

Whatever your commitment, declare it out loud or write it down, in order to cement your pledge, and take those first steps on the road to becoming a much happier and more balanced version of yourself.

MENTAL
HOUSEKEEPING

You know the feeling when you've just finished cleaning, tidying, and vacuuming the house in time for guests to arrive, and everything is arranged the way you like it? You stand back and experience a deep sense of satisfaction.

Just because the clutter isn't visible on the outside, mental housekeeping is no less important. Keeping on top of your mental housekeeping is as vital to that sense of well-being and satisfaction as keeping your home uncluttered. After all, a tidy mind is a calm mind.

BE KIND
TO YOURSELF

WHEN YOUR
MIND IS CALM,

THE PATH AHEAD
BECOMES CLEAR

INHALE DEEPLY,

EXHALE SLOWLY,

REPEAT

Happiness
is a place
between
too little and
too much.

FINNISH PROVERB

HAVE
PATIENCE

Tidying your mind is an ongoing process that takes time, so be open to embracing this as a gradual path of enlightenment. This may sound grandiose, but unlearning bad habits and relearning a healthier way of approaching your life can feel enormously liberating. Keeping your mind in good balance is a lifelong journey that will have its ups and downs—but underlying that knowledge is the awareness that you are empowered and taking control.

YOU ARE
IN CONTROL
OF YOUR LIFE

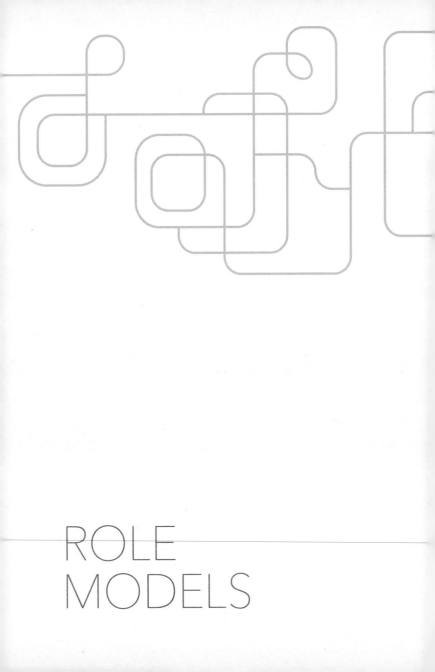

ROLE
MODELS

As you embark on your journey to mental clarity, role models can help to steer and guide you. Think of someone who seems to have mastered the art of keeping calm; an individual who appears in control of their mind. It could be someone you know, someone famous, a yoga teacher or spiritual leader, or even a historical figure. What is it about them that strikes you as grounded and clear-thinking? Speak to them if you can, to ask about their lifestyle and practices, or read a biography of the person. How did they achieve this state? Can you emulate this in your own life?

Sometimes, a single insight or piece of advice can inspire you, and by applying the same principle to your own life, you can start to make your own mind tidier and more streamlined. It can also be reassuring to learn that even the most grounded people have been through periods in their lives when they've felt overwhelmed and unable to think clearly. Remember, tidying your mind is always possible.

FOCUS
ON WHAT
MATTERS
MOST

TIDY DOESN'T MEAN EMPTY!

If you're concerned that tidying your mind might strip away the fun, the personality, or the things that make you uniquely you, don't panic—it won't. By tidying your mind, you are simply addressing the thoughts, worries, and fears that clog up your clear thinking, leaving you better able to enjoy life. Imagine your mind is a room that you wish to tidy. You might remove the clutter, but you'd keep the furniture you love and need—your bed, a comfy chair, a table to eat at. These things are good—you don't want to completely gut your room! You simply want to tidy up the things that are making the space feel messy, crowded, and unmanageable.

33

BENEFITS
OF A
TIDY MIND

The benefits of a tidy mind are manifold. You feel more capable and in control of your life. You feel calmer and therefore your mood tends to lift. You can think more clearly, concentrate well, perform your work not only more quickly but to a higher standard, and you experience more joy in life. That clogged-up feeling has gone. Like a newly serviced machine, your cogs are clean and everything's working more efficiently than a Swiss clock!

How amazing does this sound? This is what a tidy mind feels like, and it can lead to a more contented, focused you, with the energy to do the things you enjoy and time to devote to the important people in your life—yourself included. You'll probably even look and feel healthier and find yourself smiling more. So read on to find out how to get there and reap these benefits!

SATISFACTION IS AN INSIDE JOB

CHAPTER TWO

GET TO KNOW YOUR MIND

It's easy to get bogged down by clutter in the mind: the feeling that you're always behind and can never seem to finish anything before a new raft of tasks washes in; or that pervasive sense of overwhelm. However, it doesn't have to be this way. You have the power to manage your mental clutter . . . and the first step is to identify what's causing the clutter in the first place. This chapter will help you understand what's causing your stress, so that you can begin to identify your triggers and tidy your mind.

DO A
"BRAIN
DUMP"

Brain dumping is an effective technique to help tackle overthinking and work out where your mental clutter is coming from.

In a notebook, write down how you're feeling and anything else on your mind. Think about the things covered in Chapter One and consider which points resonate. Do you find yourself procrastinating, do you have an ever-growing to-do list, or do you feel you're trying to juggle too many things at once? Is there a particular aspect of your life—a feature of your job, or a person, for example—that is at the root of many of your worries? Now devote some time to reading over what you've written. Are there any dominant issues or themes that keep cropping up? This will help you to build up a clearer picture of what is causing you to feel cluttered.

Brain dumping is also useful to offload all the thoughts that are cluttering your mind. This can help you avoid rumination and guide you to focus on today's tasks, instead of being preoccupied with tomorrow's.

ASK A FRIEND

If identifying your mental clutter feels like a daunting task, why not discuss it with a friend or family member? Talking things through with someone you trust can help you work out what's at the root of your anxiety, fuzzy thinking, or fatigue. Someone who knows you well may have insights into your longer- and shorter-term behaviors to help spot which areas of your life you need to examine. It can also be encouraging to know you have the support of a loved one and can help you to feel accountable when working through the process.

YOU ARE TRYING YOUR BEST, AND THAT IS ENOUGH

The space in
which we live
should be for
the person we

are becoming now, not for the person we were in the past.

MARIE KONDO

IS THERE
A PATTERN?

Think about the situations when you tend to feel most stressed or clogged up. Is there a particular day of the week or time when you are most affected, or are your cluttered feelings at their strongest in a particular setting or environment? This may help you to see if there is a pattern and may help you to further identify the primary sources of your clutter—whether that's an activity, a group of people, an aspect of your work, or something else.

The first step to spending your time better is knowing how you're spending it now.

LAURA VANDERKAM

SHOULD, SHOULD, SHOULD

When it comes to mental clutter, language is important. How often do you catch yourself starting sentences with "I should"? "Should" implies you have to do something, even if you don't want to, which can add a layer of stress and additional clutter to your thinking. If you have a lot of "shoulds" cluttering your mind, they can weigh you down mentally and make you feel permanently unsettled and unsatisfied. More often than not, these "shoulds" are a sign you are expecting too much of yourself. So take the pressure off: are there any "shoulds" that you can simply dismiss?

TRUST IN YOUR OWN WISDOM

ALLOW
YOURSELF
TO FEEL

Suppressing or ignoring your feelings can increase your mental clutter. Similarly, wishing you felt differently (for example, feeling as though you should be happy) only adds a layer of emotional weight, which increases the clutter and stress. Allowing yourself time to reflect on your feelings gives you the space to untangle some of the more difficult feelings and emotions and can help you see yourself and your mind more clearly. Trying to fight negative thoughts and feelings tends to make them worse. Instead, allow yourself to acknowledge everything you feel, then let it pass—it can be hugely liberating.

Embrace your
emotions and
be proud of
what you feel.

DEMI LOVATO

HAVE A CONVERSATION WITH YOUR FUTURE SELF

AND ASK THEM
WHAT REALLY
MATTERS

KNOW
YOURSELF

Take some time to examine your behaviors and habits.
Often, you can make some small changes that will
help to declutter a corner of your mind. Do you often
find yourself bogged down with admin or glued to
social media for an hour when you only intended to
be online for five minutes? Perhaps you inadvertently
say yes to everybody's requests, or you have loads of
hobbies (great!) and it's resulting in too many weekly
commitments. Spending a little time facing up to the
cause of your mental clutter is a great starting point
when it comes to tidying your mind.

Incredible change happens in your life when you decide to take control of what you do have power over instead of craving control over what you don't.

STEVE MARABOLI

ARE YOU ASKING TOO MUCH OF YOURSELF?

What are your expectations of yourself? Do you expect to be able to single-handedly manage all the household admin and keep an immaculate home, for example? Consider this for a few moments, then ask yourself: are these expectations reasonable? Would you expect the same of a friend or family member? Often, people can be forgiving and generous toward others but can have unreasonable and unrealistic expectations of themselves. Cutting yourself a little slack doesn't equate to a lowering of standards. You can still have high standards but be kinder to yourself.

TREAT
YOURSELF
AS YOU WOULD
YOUR CLOSEST
FRIEND

Let go or be dragged.

ZEN PROVERB

FACE
YOUR
ANXIETIES

Next time you're feeling on edge, sit with your anxiety and gently ask yourself where it's coming from. Are you worrying about an event in the future, or are you ruminating on things you wish you hadn't said or done? This can help you to understand how your mind works, so you will become better able to recognize the kinds of things that contribute to your mental clutter.

SIMPLIFY YOUR LIFE; CLEAR YOUR MIND

CONSERVE YOUR ENERGY

How much energy are you assigning to different times of your day? If a particular part of the day is taking up more energy than it should, it's a red flag that it could be contributing to your mental clutter. Think of your energy as a piggy-bank or pot. Take control over how you choose to allocate your energy and spend it wisely. Don't let other people spill or waste your energy. Think of it as budgeting—it's your life and it's up to you how you spend it. Always keep some reserve funds in your energy bank, too—you want to safeguard your pot of energy, so you don't spread yourself too thinly!

When I win and
when I lose, I
take ownership of
it because I really
am in charge
of what I do.

NICKI MINAJ

CHAPTER THREE

HOW TO
TIDY YOUR
MIND

Now that you've spent a little time figuring out where your mental clutter has come from, it's time to roll up your sleeves and get to work! This chapter will give you some ideas and tips to help you tackle your clutter and show it who's boss! Read on to learn how to write an effective to-do list, set up healthy habits, become more purposeful, embrace active decision-making, and schedule in time for the things you love. Embracing these techniques will not only help you tidy your mind but will stop it from getting quite so cluttered in future.

We are who we choose to be.

WILL SMITH

IT'S TIME TO TAKE OWNERSHIP OF YOUR DECISIONS

AUDIT
YOUR
ACTIVITIES

Consider your average week. Write down all the activities and commitments you have—both work and social—for yourself and any dependents.

Next, divide these into three columns: things you feel positive about and that add something to your life; things you feel neutral about; and things you see as a negative or draining aspect of your week.

Of the things you feel neutral or negative about, are there any you can cut out of your life completely, delegate, or shift to a more suitable time? Of the remaining neutral or negative items, can you find a way to approach them from a more positive mindset and shift them into your positive column?

Even if you manage to cut, share, or change the way you think about just one or two tasks that you are currently viewing as stressful or a chore, it can make you feel physically lighter and will free up some mental space. Be grateful for that space and safeguard it.

Continue with this habit of prioritizing the things you enjoy in life and managing the things you don't—it's a vital life skill and one that will help you keep your mental house in order!

Gain control
of your time,
and you will
gain control
of your life.

JOHN LANDIS MASON

WRITE
A LIST

If you always seem to have multiple tasks floating around in your head, lists can be your friend. Writing a to-do list gets all that clutter out of your mind and onto a page. Grade each item on your list from most to least important, then highlight a manageable number of items from your list to prioritize. You could commit to tackling three items a day, for example. Completing the tasks and then checking them off is hugely helpful for tidying your mind. For a more detailed to-do list technique, turn the page!

AN
EFFECTIVE
TO-DO LIST
TECHNIQUE

The best way to approach to-do lists is to create a system, rather than having scraps of paper with hastily scribbled lists lying around the house. Keep a master list in a specific location, so you can always find it.

Choose a few items from your master list to tackle every week, remembering not to overload yourself. Always set aside time for enjoyable activities or relaxation.

For each task, give yourself a reasonable time limit. This means you won't be tempted to spend an excessive number of hours on something that really doesn't warrant that much of your precious time. Setting deadlines helps to keep you on track with making optimum use of each and every day, and spending too long on a task often doesn't yield better results. If you've heard of the 80/20 rule, or the Pareto Principle, it's that 80 percent of useful outcomes emerge from 20 percent effort. Heed this rule by learning when it's time to end a task and move on!

Life is short,
and it is here
to be lived.

SCHEDULE
TIME FOR
DAILY ADMIN

Compartmentalizing similar tasks can help to tidy the clutter in your mind. For example, one of the simplest ways you can do this is to set aside an hour (or even half an hour) each day to reply to emails and messages. By making this a daily ritual, you avoid a pile of admin that slowly builds, becoming a source of stress and dread. If you deal with everything daily, in small, manageable chunks of time, you gain a sense of control and organization in your life.

TRY
JOURNALING

Many people find it cathartic to write down their feelings at the end of each day. It's a helpful way to process their worries, so they can drift off into a restorative sleep instead of lying awake fretting about something. Investing in a really nice journal can be a great way to make this nightly ritual feel special—a gift you are giving yourself. Doing this also signifies that there is value in expressing your thoughts. If you prefer morning creativity, try writing for five minutes when you wake up each day.

YOU ARE
THE CEO
OF YOUR
OWN LIFE

FIND
A SYSTEM

The reason why journaling and to-do lists are such effective stress-relievers is that they help to clear the mind, thus creating a sense of calm. They also provide a framework for addressing mental clutter. Getting thoughts down on paper is the first step—the idea is to uncritically record whatever's on your mind. After that, you can find your own way to order the items written down. Which tasks are urgent, which are important, and which are irrelevant at the moment? You might postpone a long-term goal, for example, and note it in your calendar in a year's time.

Next, consider which things you can do something about and which you have no power over. Acknowledge the fact that the items you have no control over have no place clogging up your mind. Instead, think about the things you can do something about. Plan how and when you will address these.

Finally, you could sort your journal or to-do list items into standalone tasks that you can schedule in. Tasks that require more time or involve several steps—such as undertaking a course or buying a house—will require planning. Find a system that works for you to classify—and then tackle—the items that require action, within a manageable timeframe.

STREAMLINE YOUR ONLINE LIFE

There's no denying it can be challenging to keep on top of life admin, and we all have times when things seem to be spinning out of control. Many tasks require our attention—bills to pay, shopping to do, meals to cook, emails to reply to, applications to complete, contracts to cancel, petitions to sign, assignment deadlines to meet, somebody to sponsor, consent forms to complete—a seemingly never-ending flow of admin for work, school, and home.

These very simple tips will help to reduce the amount of life admin that steals your time (and clutters your mind):

1   Unsubscribe from all mailing lists you no longer wish to receive—they clog up your mind and serve no useful purpose.

2   Inform your postal worker you don't want unsolicited mail (in many countries, you can register to opt out of mass mail-outs and marketing calls).

3   Don't check work emails on days off (if this is possible in your job). It can be good to remove emails from your phone completely, so that you're not tempted to check them. Remember: your mind is craving a break!

4   Turn off notifications on your phone—instead, choose when you wish to check emails and social media (and stick to these times), so you're in control of them rather than letting them control you.

5 When you're on vacation, set up an out-of-office reply and don't be tempted to check your work emails unless you have to—or be strict with yourself and check it just twice a week. Constantly waiting for emails and messages is a known stressor—you're not allowing your mind to relax.

6 Switch your phone to airplane mode or silent when you don't want to be interrupted or distracted.

7 Check how long you're spending on various apps. If you seem to be spending too much time on an app that is serving no useful purpose, consider removing it from your phone.

These simple measures will help you to regain control over your own time and calm your racing mind.

TAKING CONTROL OF YOUR LIFE ALLOWS SPACE FOR BALANCE AND JOY

MAKE YOUR
TIME WORK
FOR YOU

The term "time poor" has grown in popularity in recent years, yet there are 168 hours in every week. That's quite a number of hours, and it can be difficult to fathom how we manage to fill them all without even realizing—often with the feeling that we haven't achieved much. If the average person needs eight hours' sleep, that's still 112 hours of waking time.

Think about how you spend those hours. Write down everything you do in an average week, working out how much time you devote to different activities each day, including leisure time. Are you happy with where your time is going? If not, next week choose to spend an extra hour or two on the things that are most important to you. If you can, schedule them into your weekly timetable.

Budgeting your time like this is a great way to start feeling "time rich." Even if you have many responsibilities and dependents, you may be able to make some small tweaks and adjustments. By spending your time in the best way possible, according to your life and commitments, you'll gain a renewed sense of positivity and joy, which can help to counter the overwhelm often associated with a cluttered mind.

All we have
to decide is
what to do

with the
time that is
given us.

J. R. R. TOLKIEN

DO A SOCIAL MEDIA DETOX

How often do you check social media? Do you ever glance at the clock and realize you've just lost three hours to the black hole of scrolling—and you'll never get them back? If this rings true, you could start imposing limits on yourself so you're making better use of your time. For example, you could check social media every Monday and Thursday, or allow yourself a half-hour window each morning. Regulating your social media use in this way is a great idea to try if you feel like you never have enough hours to get things done—cutting back can really help to make your day feel more spacious and your mind calmer.

When people
will not weed
their own
minds, they
are apt to
be overrun
by nettles.

HORACE WALPOLE

ALLOCATE
YOUR ENERGY
WITH PURPOSE
AND AWARENESS

Do not forget
your duty to
love yourself.

SØREN KIERKEGAARD

BRAIN DECLUTTERING

Have you ever done a clear-out of your bedroom or garage and donated or thrown away unwanted items? If so, you will know how therapeutic this can feel.

Just as a clear-out involves sorting and assessing what you wish to keep and what you wish to discard, brain dumping helps you discard the thoughts that are cluttering your mind. Writing down whatever is on your mind immediately relieves your brain of having to keep that thought or task at the front. Brain dumping is something you can do regularly to keep your mind uncluttered.

YOUR TIME IS
PRECIOUS:
USE IT WELL

CREATE
A GRID

This can be a nice idea if you'd like to keep all your musings and tasks in one place. To begin, divide a sheet of paper (or a page of your journal) into three sections. Label the left-hand box "Thoughts," the middle box "To do," and the right-hand box "Top three priorities."

Filling in the grid each day—and then taking action on these items—will help you to process and resolve some of the things contributing to your congested mind and can help to reduce any related stress and anxiety.

THOUGHTS	TO DO	TOP THREE PRIORITIES
Note your thoughts	List the day's tasks	Rewrite the top three items from your to-do list here—and plan when you will do them

EMBRACE ACTIVE DECISION-MAKING

If you're someone who gets flustered when decisions pile up and need to be made, commit to taking control of the process. Major decisions require time and thought, but many minor decisions don't actually matter. Consider the decision that needs to be made, assess the options, as well as the pros and cons of each choice, make your best decision based on the information available, and then move on. We learn from all of our decisions, so even if you later think you made an incorrect or ill-judged choice, this will inform your thought process next time.

You only need one ray of light to chase all the shadows away.

RESPOND,
DON'T REACT

While the same mishap might happen to two people, one of them might react negatively, in a state of panic or anger, while the other person might be able to remain calm, taking it in their stride and considering their options before responding accordingly.

It's worth spending a little time learning how to achieve that underlying sense of calm in the face of unexpected or unwanted events. Learning to manage your reactions, and being able to mentally pause for a moment before responding, will help you avoid hitting that stage where your mind feels like a messy, uncontrollable scribble.

You can learn to emulate that. When you catch yourself reacting negatively to a situation—whether that's falling into a state of panic or launching into an uncontrolled outburst of rage—pause for a moment and count to ten slowly. Acknowledge that you—and only you— are in charge of your behavior, and the way in which you respond to a situation is a choice, no matter how challenging that situation might seem on the outside. Practicing a calmer response and learning to control your behavior, rather than being a passive observer of your actions, can be hugely empowering—and a calm mind is a tidy mind. Instead of kicking out with involuntary knee-jerk reactions, learn to gradually straighten that knee.

TRY SINGLE-TASKING

If you've identified that your mental clutter comes from trying to do too many things at once, try single-tasking. Focusing on one task at a time, with purpose, is more effective than juggling multiple things at once. Giving your full attention to a single task means you're able to concentrate on completing that task to the best of your ability. You achieve closure and can then move on to another task. Attempting to multitask—switching back and forth between various jobs—makes it impossible to give your full attention to anything, causing an accumulation of stress in the mind.

CELEBRATE YOUR STRENGTHS

CREATE
HEALTHY
HABITS

What are the things in your day that take up time, space, and energy? You might think of them as chores. If food shopping and cooking meals leave you frustrated, then try a new system to see if it works for you. Drawing up a weekly meal plan and then shopping accordingly might be just the adjustment that will help to shift this from something you see as a negative into something perfectly manageable. Or perhaps you might like to listen to a podcast or audiobook while you cook—it can feel wonderfully satisfying to "read" for half an hour and cook a family dinner at the same time!

If keeping your house tidy is more of an issue, what can you do about it? Can you draw up a chore chart so the work is done and shared? Or how about tackling it with a friend, then returning the favor and helping them tidy theirs? Whatever issues you identify as contributing to your mental clutter, aim to work out what steps you can take to reduce these.

DO IT, SCHEDULE IT, SKIP IT, OR SHARE IT . . .

JUST TRY
NOT TO
OVERTHINK IT!

DECLUTTER YOUR PHYSICAL SPACE

Making your home free from clutter is another simple yet effective step that will help contribute to a calmer, clearer mind. Physical clutter can signal that something needs to be dealt with, disturbing your inner peace, so it can be hugely therapeutic to sort through a room and donate, upcycle, recycle, or get rid of unwanted items.

Accumulating vast numbers of possessions is a relatively recent human behavior. To prevent possessions morphing into clutter, make tidying things away a habit. Think: clutter-free space, clutter-free mind!

If you run into a wall, don't turn around and give up. Figure out how to climb it, go through it, or work around it.

SHERYL CROW

TAKE
REGULAR
BREAKS

Regular breaks are excellent not only for structuring your day, but also for providing respite and a change of focus from your main activity. Invest in your own well-being and take a full lunch break. If your work culture is an unhealthy one that equates this with laziness, be the courageous person who breaks that unhelpful taboo. Meeting a friend for a brisk walk, sitting in a park, or supporting a local café can be just the respite you need, leaving you able to return to your work feeling refreshed and energized.

YOU ARE CAPABLE; YOU ARE CALM

CULTIVATE
A HEALTHY
MINDSET

It's all very well auditing our time, but for some people it's simply not possible to drop various commitments and magically create an extra hour every day, or even every week. A single parent working full-time on a low income, for example, supplemented by a second job, may find the idea of extra time a luxury they simply can't access. One thing we do have the ability to change, however—regardless of our economic situation or how busy we are—is our mindset.

Observe your mindset about particular stressors. For example, instead of feeling vexed about having to complete a report for work, needing to wash the dishes, fill in a form, or care for someone, can you choose a more positive attitude of gratitude, and be glad you have these things in your life, needing your care and attention? Can you choose to see essential actions for a desirable outcome simply as "life" instead of "chores"? For example, cleaning dishes means you enjoy a tidy kitchen, and caring for a child means you benefit from that unique relationship. Sometimes, simply changing our attitude to an activity or commitment can make a huge difference, and we come to view it as an enriching, rather than draining, aspect of our life.

Just when you feel you have no time to relax, know that this is the moment you most need to make time to relax.

MATT HAIG

SCHEDULE IN SOME ME-TIME

No doubt you will be familiar with the proverb, "All work and no play makes Jack a dull boy." Yet how often do you heed this age-old advice? Making time for the things you love is enormously important. Scheduling in me-time is like feeding your soul—and even a small amount of food for your soul will be gratefully consumed. You'll feel the benefits and sustenance long after the event, which will leave you with more positive energy to go about your daily life.

ACCEPT
THIS MOMENT
EXACTLY AS IT IS

REALISTIC GOAL-SETTING

Striving for unattainable goals yields no winners: it just makes people feel they can never achieve these high standards, resulting in a chronic sense of failure and anxiety. So, when you set your own goals, make them realistic. Reject any pressure to be "perfect"— perfectionism is your foe; acceptance is your friend. This doesn't mean you can't have high standards; of course you can. It's not about lowering or abandoning standards; it's about setting achievable goals. In doing so, you will remove any related pressure and anxiety from your mind, helping you to stay focused and calm.

I am the sole
author of the
dictionary that
defines me.

ZADIE SMITH

CHAPTER FOUR

KEEPING YOUR MIND TIDY

Just as important as knowing how to tidy your mind is being able to keep it tidy. Prevention, as they say, is often better than cure, so embracing good habits for keeping your mind organized and clear from clutter will help you live a calmer and more purposeful life. This chapter explores healthy habits you can adopt to keep your stress in check and protect your well-being in the future. After all, keeping our minds in good balance is a lifelong process.

TRY MINI
MEDITATIONS

If your mind has been feeling frazzled lately, one of the simplest and most effective things you can do is to try daily mini meditations. Even if you think you're excessively busy, you can perform these short meditations regularly, even if you only have twenty seconds. Practicing daily meditation has been shown to reduce stress, improve memory and concentration, boost mental health and sleep quality, and lower blood pressure. And if you think you don't have time, that's probably a sign you could benefit a lot from its calming effects!

To get started, do an internet search to find a guided mini meditation that suits you, or try a few. The general idea is to focus on a single thing, such as a color, a sensation, an object, or your breath. Channeling your focus for a few moments can act like a reset button for your mind.

Mini meditations can be performed anywhere you have a few moments of time—on a train, in an elevator, or waiting in line . . . even while you brush your teeth! Try it today—it could be just the tonic for a tidier mind.

REGULAR
SELF-CARE

Self-care isn't just a bandage for difficult times; turning it into a regular, daily habit can improve your overall mental and emotional wellbeing. Self-care will mean different things to different people: for some, it might be putting aside an hour for a bath with aromatherapy candles or for a yoga sequence; for others, it could be playing sport, reading, going for a woodland walk, or a video call with a friend. The trick is to make these nurturing things part of your daily and weekly schedule to ensure there's space in your life for you.

Simplicity is the ultimate sophistication.

LEONARDO DA VINCI

LISTEN TO YOUR BODY

When you're feeling a little tired or run down, try to take it easy for a few days. It's OK to skip a weekly commitment sometimes if you're tired and just need to rest. Other animals hibernate to conserve energy; sometimes you might feel like that, too! Listening to your body when it's telling you it's tired means you're investing in your health and well-being, and switching off for a day or two can also lower your stress levels. Think of it as essential preventative care and ongoing maintenance—just like a gardener or mechanic might do.

THIS DAY IS A GIFT—
EMBRACE IT

IT'S OK
TO SAY
"NO"

Many of us are socially conditioned into wanting to be helpful. This is wonderful, of course, until it begins to negatively impact our own energy and joy and affect our capacity to run our own lives effectively. If you wish to tidy your mind, you'll need to become comfortable with saying "no" sometimes. If you're the sort of person who is always obliging, it might feel a little strange at first, but you'll soon discover it can be empowering and liberating to say "no" to some things, especially if you have a lot on your plate already.

Other people tend to respect those who value their own time—and when you do consciously say "yes" to something in the future, it means you'll be giving your time willingly and on your own terms, making your offer of help all the more sincere.

When someone asks you to do something, spend a little time considering before you commit. If it feels like something you can contribute to constructively and positively, say "yes." But if the task is going to feel draining or like a duty, it's OK to say "no."

Saying "no" does not always show a lack of generosity

and saying "yes"
is not always
a virtue.

PAULO COELHO

PRACTICE
MINDFULNESS

Mindfulness is about paying attention to the present moment. Learning to focus on your senses and notice the world around and within you is proven to improve mental clarity and mood and can help you to rediscover purpose in your life. This simple skill is recognized by national health organizations around the world as helping combat an array of conditions, from depression and anxiety to postnatal health and weight management.

Let thoughts go, observe sensations, and bring your attention to the moment. Practicing this for a few minutes every day will help you to find long-term clarity.

Stop valuing other people's time more than yours.

AVERY BLANK

GREEN
THERAPY

Time spent outside in a green space, such as a park or garden, is a proven mood enhancer. Spending just two hours a week in a natural setting has been linked to better health and well-being. Green spaces help to reconnect us to nature and offer a raft of benefits, including boosted immunity, improved cardiovascular health, stress reduction, enhanced mood, and greater longevity. Making this a regular commitment will work wonders for keeping your mind in good shape.

YOU
DESERVE
YOUR OWN
LOVE

MAKE AN APPOINTMENT WITH YOURSELF

One of the nicest things you can do for your own well-being is to clear an empty space in your calendar and make an appointment with yourself—the idea being that you will be free to use that time however you wish on the day! Scheduling in a big blank space might feel radical, but devoting even a small window of time to yourself is incredibly valuable. You will reap the rewards long after in increased joy and energy, and it will rub off on those around you, too.

Time for yourself matters and this appointment with yourself is as important as everything else in your calendar, so treat it with the same level of commitment you give to other meetings and events. Even when you're feeling time-poor and overburdened, making space for yourself can help your mind feel rested and clear.

YOU CAN'T PLEASE EVERYONE

It's impossible to please everyone. Each person has their own preferences and opinions, likes and dislikes, and what pleases one will displease another. See this as something that adds interest and variety to life, and accept that you can't satisfy everyone; that's their own responsibility. Simply try to follow your own heart. Being true to yourself will help you to maintain an authentic sense of well-being and self-respect.

I have just
three things to
teach: simplicity,
patience,
compassion.
These three are
your greatest
treasures.

LAO TZU

BE YOUR OWN PERSON

Don't try to be someone you're not or live by another person's standards (those standards could be exacting or sloppy—either way, they're not right for you). Set your own benchmark and live by your own moral and ethical code—then you'll naturally respect yourself. Practice being kind and reasonable with yourself, and regulate negative self-talk. If a critical voice in your head tries to put you down, counter it with something more constructive in order to keep your mind positive and clear.

SMILING MAKES
EVERYONE FEEL
BETTER—YOURSELF
INCLUDED

HEALTHY
BODY,
HEALTHY
MIND

One way to approach your mind is to understand that it is part of the whole that is you. Your mind and body are one and the same. Taking some time to reconnect with your body can also help to ease stress and calm the mind.

To do this, find a comfortable spot and mentally scan your body. Breathe slowly and deeply, and focus your attention on any areas of discomfort. After your body scan, you could stretch gently into any areas of tension. Try not to rush: in this time-poor world, you are feeding yourself with some nutritious time!

It's also important to prioritize quality sleep habits, such as a calm bedtime routine, a reduction in bright lighting and stimulants in the evening, and making sure you leave space for a regular eight hours of sleep every night. And getting plenty of exercise in fresh air is key. A walk in the woods or alongside water, for example, are both proven to have significant mental health benefits and can help to clear your mind. You can then return to your day with increased mental clarity, energy, and joy.

YOU ARE WORTHY OF

YOUR
OWN
BEST
EFFORTS

A HEALTHY DIET FOR A HEALTHY MIND

The food on your plate nourishes not just your body but your mind, too, so it's important to be conscious of what you eat. Consider upping your intake of nourishing foods—think fresh vegetables, beans and legumes, lean meats, fish, eggs, and plenty of healthy nuts, seeds, and oils. Drink plenty of water to keep yourself hydrated, too. And remember, a diet that's high in sugars, simple carbohydrates, and processed foods may contribute to brain fog, so aim to keep these to a minimum—you'll soon notice a difference in how you feel.

You have to know
that as long as
you love who you
are—your morals,
your values,
that type of stuff
—you're OK.

NICKI MINAJ

SPEND TIME WITH YOUR TRIBE

Arrange to spend time with the important people in your life—the ones whose company you enjoy. Sometimes feeling swamped is simply a sign that you've lost a little balance, so it's time to tip the scales back toward the fun, positive side of you. Spending time with people you love is an easy way to do this, so think of those who bring out your joyful, carefree side and organize a good-for-the-soul get-together.

FRIENDS HELP
TO CREATE JOY
TO CHERISH
AND SHARE

Acknowledge
all of your small
victories. They will
eventually add up to
something great.

KARA GOUCHER

STAY GRATEFUL

Spend a little time each day thinking about the things in life you're grateful for—it could be as small as a beautiful sunrise or a warming cup of tea. Write down one thing you're most thankful for at the end of each day and put it in a jar. You could decorate the jar to make it an appealing part of your day that you look forward to. Whenever you're feeling in need of a lift, pick out a few of your thoughts and you will feel grateful all over again!

YOU HAVE
THE COURAGE
TO SEEK
SOLUTIONS—
TRUST YOUR
JUDGMENT

YOU ARE A BORN PROBLEM-SOLVER

SEEKING
HELP

If you're struggling with anxiety, depression, or a sense of overwhelm, it's OK to ask for help. Who are your support crew—the people in your life who believe in you and make you feel good about yourself? In times of stress, reach out to them.

If you live with other people, ask them to take on a greater proportion of household tasks. Tell your partner, children, relatives, or housemates that you're struggling and need more help from them. It's healthy to ask for assistance when you need it.

If your work is a source of stress, speak to your boss or HR department and ask for support or extra time to complete tasks. Or if a daily commute leaves you exhausted, is there another way or time to travel—or can you ask to work some days from home?

If you're still struggling, or feel as though you're experiencing symptoms of anxiety or depression, it's a good idea to seek professional help. Make an appointment with your doctor or therapist, or you could call a helpline if you wish to remain anonymous. There are people and services out there who are trained to help in times of mental unrest—check out mentalhealth. gov—so never be afraid to ask for help.

You just have to trust yourself.

BEYONCÉ

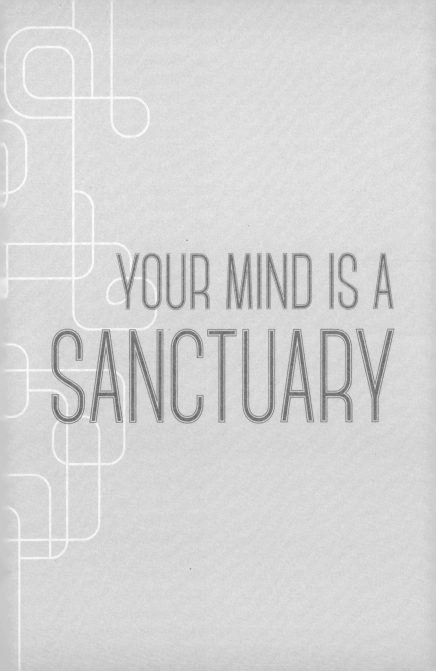

YOUR MIND IS A
SANCTUARY

CONCLUSION

SO, LET'S GET TIDYING!

Hopefully this book has given you some ideas and inspiration on how to begin tidying your mind and maintaining a regular decluttering schedule. The aim is comfortable mental space, not house clearance or zero clutter. It's simply about finding balance, control, purpose, and joy. Learn how to budget your time and energy, and enjoy the process of getting to know your mind a little better, so you can find your own way to make it clearer and calmer—it's an incredible place that deserves your care and respect!